The Dur Alone At The Edge

Rod Langley

Talonbooks   •   Vancouver   •   1991

Published with assistance from the Canada Council.

Talonbooks
201 - 1019 East Cordova Street
Vancouver
British Columbia V6A 1M8
Canada

This book was designed by Sally Bryer Mennell, typeset in 11/12 point Palacio by Pièce de Résistance Ltée., and printed in Canada by Hignell Printing Ltd.

First printing: September 1991

Canadian Cataloguing in Publication Data

Langley, Rod, 1942–
    The Dunsmuirs: alone at the edge

    A play.
    ISBN 0-88922-297-5
    1. Dunsmuir, Robert, 1825-1889—Drama.
2. Dunsmuir family—Drama. I. Title.
PS8573.A54D8 1991   C812'.54   C91-091489-3
PR9199.3.L324D8 1991

The Dunsmuirs was first performed at The Nanaimo Festival July 15 - August 21, 1988 with the following cast:

Susan Hamilton	Corinne Hebden
Robert Dunsmuir	Barry MacGregor
Joan Dunsmuir	Kate Robbins
Stuart, Smithers	Roark Critchlow
Meakin, Jock Hamilton	Don Wallace
Alex Dunsmuir	Peter Outerbridge
James Dunsmuir	Daryl Shuttleworth
Lieutenant Diggle	Keith Martin Gordey

Directed by Bindon Kinghorn. Set designed by Ross Nichol. Costumes designed by Christine Kinghorn. Lighting designed by Bert Timmermans.
The playwright wishes to thank Duncan Fraser and Kathie Bradshaw for their assistance in the presentation of the script.

The Dunsmuir Chronicles were performed at The Nanaimo Festival with the following casts:

Alone at the Edge of the Earth:		*A Promise Kept:*
The Dunsmuirs, Part 1		*The Dunsmuirs, Part II*
May 24-31, 1989		June 7-21, 1989
Patti Allan	Joan	Joan
Tony Bancroft	Meakin, Diggle	Pinkerton's Man, Doctor
Ron Halder	James	James
Annabel Kershaw	Susan	Josephine
David Marr	Alex	Alex
John Nolan	Stuart, Smithers, miner	Wally, clergyman
Ric Read	Robbie	Robbie
Don Wallace	Hamilton, miner	Sir John A. MacDonald
Louise Whitney	miner's wife	

Extras: Chad Hartel, David Froom, Dominique Denis, Jean Medland.
Stage manager Angela Beaulieu.

Directed by Duncan Fraser. Assistant Director Tony Bancroft.
Set and lighting designed by Paul Williams. Costumes designed by Margaret Perry and Irene Pieper. Sound designer Scott Littlejohn (Intimate Sounds Recording Studio.)

CHARACTERS
NOTE: Actors are free to use Scottish accents at their own discretion.

ROBERT DUNSMUIR (ROBBIE)

JOAN DUNSMUIR

STUART

MEAKIN

ALEX DUNSMUIR

JAMES DUNSMUIR

SUSAN HAMILTON

JOCK HAMILTON

SMITHERS

LIEUTENANT DIGGLE

MINERS

Act One

SCENE ONE

The play begins in total blackness. We are down the mine. There is the drip of water, the occasional creak of timbering and the sound of a distant pick-axe. Slow footsteps echo closer, then stop. A heavily accented Scottish voice cries "Dunsmuir! Robbie Dunsmuir — are ye there?" *The pick-axing ceases.* "Up top, laddie, yer papers are come, yer away to Canada."

The sound of Robbie running towards us as the creak of mine timbers becomes the squeak of rigging and ships' timbers.

SCENE TWO

On the deck of the Barque, Pekin.

Sound: Squeak of rigging. Sea etc. Lights up on JOAN, on the deck.

ROBBIE: *(Calling off)*
    Joan! Joan!

JOAN:
    Here!

ROBBIE: *(appears)*
    Get below, you'll freeze up here.

JOAN:
    I want to get my last glimpse of the Scottish Hills. We'll not see them again.

ROBBIE:

> Good riddance! A lot of good those hills did us —
> or our fathers — or their fathers before them. I'll
> no' look back. If it's a boy you carry he will not
> dig those hills for coal till he's spitting it from his
> lungs, old before his time. In the new world
> there will be a new beginning.

JOAN:

> Beginning — beginning of what? Just another coal
> mine . . . for you . . . for your sons . . . there's
> no new beginning there.

ROBBIE:

> Where we're going it will be different, you'll see.
> By God, Joan, I promise you . . . I'll succeed so
> greatly . . . I'll build you a castle . . . a fairy tale
> castle . . . we'll have horses and servants. Yes a
> castle . . . finer than those on any loch in Scotland.

JOAN: *(Dully)*

> You're dreamin' again. Bonded for seven years to
> the Hudson's Bay Company. They own you body
> and soul.

ROBBIE:

> You'll see. I promise you. A castle. So grand it'll
> make yer father's house on the High Street look
> like a croft. *(Pause as he sees Joan's expression
> change)* Don't lass. C'mon. Come below. It
> doesn't do any good . . . . Sorry — I shouldn't
> ha' said that.

JOAN:

> They wouldn't even come and say goodbye. Do
> they hate me that much?

ROBBIE:

> It's me they hate! Anyway. Forget them. We'll
> start fresh. You'll see.

JOAN:
    It's alright for you. You left nothing behind.

ROBBIE:
    No, nothing. *(Beat)* But now for the first time I've
    got someone to talk to and share with, and I
    promise you . . . I'll make it all up to you. You'll
    never regret what happened.

JOAN:
    I'll regret it until the day I die!

ROBBIE: *(Hurt)*
    No lass.

JOAN:
    I'm sorry Robbie. I know you'll do your best.

ROBBIE:
    And my best is a castle. No less. Now come
    below.

SCENE THREE

    *Dunsmuirs' rough-hewn miner's cottage on Vancouver
    Island.*

    *Lights up on JOAN hurrying in distressed. The mine
    whistle blows three short blasts. She stops to listen.
    Then she gathers herself, dons a clean apron and works
    furiously to prepare for ROBBIE's return. Water
    simmers on the stove. ROBBIE enters, grimy from the
    mine. He stands a moment admiring her.*

ROBBIE:
    Slow down, Joanie, slow down.

JOAN: *(Startled)*
    Slow down! And who's going to feed the bairns
    and the horse and cook and clean and . . . *(Drops
    everything, sniffles)*

7

ROBBIE: *(Going to her)*
>Dinna fash yerself, lassie, what is it?

JOAN:
>I'm sorry Robbie, I don't like you to see me like
>this. You've enough to worry about down that
>pit!

ROBBIE:
>All I worry about down there is you wearing
>yourself to the bone up here. *(Beat)* Is that it —
>you just weary?

JOAN:
>I went to clean out Lady's stall just now and
>there was another bear right behind the
>woodpile. I didnae see it till it stood up. Big black
>devil. That's three already this winter. You can't
>hear them in the rain. Lord, I hate this place. I
>hate it!

ROBBIE:
>Calm down.

JOAN:
>It's purgatory here.

ROBBIE:
>Now Lass . . .

JOAN:
>Y'hear? Purgatory! Four years of Purgatory and
>another three to go before we can leave this God-
>forsaken wilderness.

ROBBIE:
>And go where?

JOAN:
>Anywhere but here. My father was right . . . it's
>the edge of the earth!

ROBBIE:

> And still not far enough for him, the toffee-nosed prig! *(JOAN gives him a look)* You know damn fine we can't go home again, Joanie, and even if we could I wouldn't want to. At least I'm an equal here.

JOAN:

> That's not saying much.

ROBBIE:

> Nanaimo is just beginning — it will grow, and change. And you and I and the bairns will grow and change with it. Be patient lass. This can be our home. A good home.

JOAN:

> Home! With no books, no music? Nothing!

ROBBIE:

> What no music? *(He begins clowning and singing)* "Oh whit a wee shirt shirt ye've got to cover yer wee behind. Oh whit a wee shirt shirt ye've got, Ye'd better pull down the blind."

JOAN: *(Can't help herself; she begins to giggle)*
> Oh Robbie.

> *He kisses her hand.*

JOAN: *(Pulling her hands away)*
> Look at them. They played the piano once.

ROBBIE:

> And they will again, you'll see. Everything'll be alright here. There will be schools in time and books and music. Meanwhile you have me to amuse you.

JOAN:

> Like the times we used to meet secretly at Aunt

Agnes' house I suppose? . . . Poor old Aunt
Agnes! She thought it was so romantic.

ROBBIE:
It was!

JOAN:
Och aye, you the wayward son of a coal miner
meeting her precious niece in secret because my
father wouldnae let you across his stoop!

ROBBIE:
What was it he used to call me?

JOAN: *(Smiling)*
The Bitter Seed.

ROBBIE: *(Laughing)*
The Bitter Seed!

JOAN: *(With a little bitterness)*
Well you got him back didn't you, Robbie!

ROBBIE: *(A long look)*
What happened was because I loved you, Joan,
you know that. I dreamed of meeting a lass
like you.

JOAN:
Aye, your dreams! You made them sound so real.
You beguiled me.

ROBBIE:
You were beguiled because my dreams were real.
Aye. Dreams were the only reality I knew, until I
met you. I love you lass. And I will not rest until
I make you a queen in this new world.

JOAN: *(Resigned)*
Oh no — not the castle.

ROBBIE:

> Believe it! *(He holds her close)* "Encircled in her clasping arms, How have the raptured moments flown: How have I wished for fortune's chorus, For her dear sake, and hers alone!" *(JOAN kisses him)*

JOAN:

> C'mon lad. Let's get the grime off. *(Pours hot water into basin)* If I can't get this house clean at least I'll keep you clean and polished. *(ROBBIE appears far away in thought)* What is it?

ROBBIE:

> I'm thinking.

JOAN:

> Aye?

ROBBIE:

> Thinking about the coal seams we've been working.

JOAN:

> Ach, I'd think you'd want to forget that at the end of your day. *(She begins washing his back)*

ROBBIE:

> Joannie . . . it's good quality coal but the seams are thin.

JOAN:

> And?

ROBBIE:

> Listen, I believe somewhere . . . somewhere near here there's a magic seam.

JOAN:

> . . . Oh really, Robbie! There you go again. *(Laughs)* A dream seam!

ROBBIE:

Aye. Magic. *(Seriously)* A seam of coal so thick and so rich, it will be magic — and I'll find it . . . it's out there and I'll find it!

JOAN:

And what would you do if you found it?

ROBBIE:

We'd be rich! Jamie and wee Alex would never have to eat, sleep and work to the tune of a mine whistle for one thing. And you m'dear would be a queen . . . in your castle.

JOAN:

Like Cinderella?

ROBBIE:

Aye.

JOAN: *(Sighing)*

But that's a fairy story.

ROBBIE:

You'll see. Tomorrow I'm going to Mr. Stuart and ask him for permission to prospect for myself . . . in my free time.

JOAN:

Free time? What free time?

ROBBIE:

On Sundays.

JOAN: *(Flaring)*

Sundays! I hardly see you for six days a week as it is! The Sabbath is for rest, not seeking riches. Don't tempt the spirit, Robbie.

ROBBIE:

Ah, Joan. That's a lot of old blather! *(Throws down cloth)*

JOAN: *(Handing him a towel)*
> God has pre-ordained what happens to us in this life! And Sunday prospecting isn't going to change it.

ROBBIE: *(Wiping)*
> Havers! Our fate is in our own hands! And that's why I'm going to talk to Stuart tomorrow.

JOAN:
> Ah, Robbie. You'll get nowhere with that one! *(Exits)*

SCENE FOUR

> *Neutral area.*

> *Sound: Mine whistle, and chug of steam engine. Then under. Lights up on STUART addressing ROBBIE.*

STUART:
> Ach, Dunsmuir, it's always something. Last time it was the foreman's job, now a free miner's license! It can't be done. You're a sound man, the best, but if we allow you to prospect on your own, everyone will want the same. Got enough trouble keeping men working in the pit, what with all these wild rumors of a gold rush in California. Listen. Work hard below for the Company and you'll find we reward loyalty.

ROBBIE:
> How?

STUART:
> An opportunity will present itself.

ROBBIE:
> That's what I've been telling my wife for four bloody years.

STUART:

    Just persevere . . . .

ROBBIE:

    Persevere! Christ, Stuart, you're just a puppet.
    They fart in London, you sniff. These seams are
    not going to last forever, you know.

STUART:

    They'll see me out.

ROBBIE:

    If I find coal, you look good in London.

STUART:

    Policy . . . . It's against policy. (*He exits*)

ROBBIE: (*Yelling after him*)

    To Hell with policy! You can't fuel a boiler with
    bloody policy!

Lights up on MEAKIN.

MEAKIN: (*To ROBBIE*)

    So the Company won't let you prospect
    Dunsmuir? Ha! What did you expect? (*Spits*)
    Look, my friend, the company owns us. We're
    indentured for years, at low wages with death
    lurking around every turn of the "drift." We're
    slaves here, man. But in other places there're free
    men prospecting for themselves — and not for
    coal either; for gold. I know you're under
    contract here, and you've got a family, but listen.
    This is the New World. They can't hold us down
    like they did in the Old Country.

Sound: Mine whistle. Miners' voices.
Cross fade to STUART.

STUART: (*To crowd*)

    Hey you lot! Before y'go down! (*Pause*) A serious
    incident took place last night. Four men ran off

from the village — and the mine. This in breach of their contracts. Consequently they are being pursued by officers of the company with guns and dogs and their families will be evicted from company homes. Let this be a warning to any others with ideas about California! *(To ROBBIE)* You're all under contract to the company, and you will remain so until your seven-year term is up!

MEAKIN:

If the company would pay us a living wage, and let us live like free men, maybe those who left would still be here!

STUART:

Those ideas smack of disloyalty, Meakin. I'd watch my tongue if I were you. *(Exits)*

MEAKIN:

Well Dunsmuir, do we hold our tongues, or do we speak up like men? *(Approaching ROBBIE)* When the shift whistle blows tomorrow we refuse to go below — unless we get a better deal. We can win but we must stick together — to a man. What do you say, Dunsmuir? Will you clan with us?

ROBBIE: *(Clasp hands)*

Why not? I'm getting nowhere with Stuart.

MEAKIN: *(Whisper)*

Then tomorrow it is.

Lights change. ROBBIE re-enters house.

SCENE FIVE

JOAN: *(Sleepily, whispering, with lantern)*

Who's that?

ROBBIE:
> Shshsh. It's me.

JOAN:
> Are you sober, man?

ROBBIE:
> Never been more sober in my life.

JOAN:
> What's going on?

ROBBIE:
> There's going to be a strike.

JOAN: *(Wide awake suddenly)*
> What?

ROBBIE:
> Meakin and the others see it as a way to get the company to bargain!

JOAN:
> Don't get mixed up with the likes of them! Look at what's happened to the families of those that listened to his wild blather. Tossed out in the wind and rain without shelter.

ROBBIE: *(Firmly)*
> If we stand together, they'll have to bargain! Here's a chance to improve our lot, Joan.

JOAN:
> Or lose what little we have.

ROBBIE:
> I've got to go along with them.

JOAN:
> Robbie, please! You've got family. It's alright for Meakin. He's single. What's he got to lose?

ROBBIE:
> Too late now. I've given my word.

JOAN:
> And if you join Meakin and you all fail? What then? First tossed out of Scotland. Now tossed out here! I should be getting used to it.

ROBBIE:
> It's a chance we'll have to take.

JOAN:
> Robbie, don't y'see? You'll not beat the company! They own the house we live in, and they own us! We must accept our lot and bide our time till the contract's up.

ROBBIE:
> Not the Company, not anyone is going to keep me on the bottom of the heap forever! *(Calms down)* Anyway, it's too late, I've given my word. If I cross the line now, I'll be a Scab.

JOAN:
> That's Meakin talkin' again.

ROBBIE:
> Look! Your father was a high and mighty merchant on the High Street. You don't know what it means to live as a scab family. Better to be dead. Do you want to be spat on in the street?

> *A knocking at the door. JOAN dons a clean apron as ROBBIE answers the door.*

ROBBIE:
> Stuart!

JOAN:
> Good evening Mr. Stuart.

STUART:
Good evening Ma'am, Dunsmuir.

JOAN:
Would you take a seat Mr. Stuart, and have a cup of tea.

ROBBIE:
Or a wee dram?

STUART:
No, thank you kindly. I just came to have a few words with Robert here, and then I'll be down the road. Perhaps another time.

JOAN:
Then I'll see to Jamie and Alex and put myself to bed if you'll excuse me.

STUART:
Certainly, Mrs. Dunsmuir. Pleasant dreams.

JOAN:
I don't dream, Mr. Stuart. My husband does the dreaming for both of us. Goodnight.

STUART looks puzzled. JOAN exits upstairs.

STUART:
Braw lass, that.

ROBBIE:
Aye.

STUART:
She keeps a neat home.

ROBBIE:
It's neat, but it isn't home to her.

STUART:
Still, it's better than nothing. There're four

wives living under the trees tonight — I'm sure
she prefers this to that.

ROBBIE:

They've been taken in already. People stick
together.

STUART:

Well if they're still sticking together tomorrow,
they'll ALL finish up in the woods.

Silence.

STUART:

All right, Dunsmuir, drop the tea and crumpets.
You know why I'm here.

ROBBIE:

Do I?

STUART:

We know what Meakin and his sheep are up to.
You'll steer clear of the lot of them if you know
what's good for you.

ROBBIE:

That so?

STUART:

Trust me man. Stand by the company tomorrow
and your loyalty . . .

ROBBIE: *(Incensed)*

You want me to scab!

STUART:

. . . will be amply rewarded.

ROBBIE:

Rewarded? How? Eh? How? I've been waiting
four bloody years to hear this!

Pause.

STUART:
Stand by us tomorrow and we'll make you foreman below.

ROBBIE: *(Laughs)*
Thanks a lot! Not only will I be a scab, but a scab foreman to boot! That's the big reward? My family treated as lepers in the village, spat on in the street? Och aye, Stuart, that's what happens. I've seen it back home. I know what I'm talking about.

STUART:
The men look up to you, Dunsmuir. You cross that line tomorrow, the rest will follow.

ROBBIE:
The way they're feeling right now, they wouldn't follow Jesus Christ across the line.

Pause.

STUART: *(Reaching into his pocket)*
See this man? It's a copy of a letter from the Company's Governors in London. They're sending out a whole shipload of miners from Staffordshire to work here. So it doesn't matter what that Ayreshire riff-raff say to you because as soon as the new people arrive, we'll get rid of that scum and no one will be the wiser. So don't worry about scab talk. Here's your chance man.

Pause.

ROBBIE:
You're sure these new people are coming?

STUART:
I'm sure.

ROBBIE:
>And they won't know about the strike?

STUART:
>My word on it! They've already left England on the Princess Royal. Be here in three months.

ROBBIE: *(Handing back the letter)*
>You're asking too much for too little.

STUART:
>My God man, what more do you want?

ROBBIE:
>You know damn fine what more I want.

>*Pause.*

STUART:
>The license.
>*(ROBBIE nods)*
>Now who's asking too much?

ROBBIE:
>Not me.

STUART:
>Why do you want it so badly?

ROBBIE:
>You wouldn't believe me if I told you. Take it or leave it.

STUART:
>You're a hard man, Robert Dunsmuir.

ROBBIE:
>That's why you're here.

>*Pause.*

STUART:
>You've got me over a barrel. Foreman and free

miner's licence? *(Pause)* Done! When you cross the line!

ROBBIE:
    IF I cross the line.

STUART:
    Jesus!

SCENE SIX

Sound: Voices of miners, agitated.

MEAKIN: *(Yelling)*
    It's our only way!

Sound: Miners in agreement.

STUART:
    Don't listen to him men. He'll lead you all to prison.

MEAKIN:
    We're already in prison, Stuart.

STUART:
    I give you one chance. Any man willing to walk over here — and go below — will be rewarded for his loyalty. Is there not a man who has the balls and common decency to honor the contract he put his hand to? Well? Is there?

ROBBIE steps up. Noise abates. Whispers of "Dunsmuir" etc.

MEAKIN:
    YOU BLOODY RAT!

The voices of the men yelling "SCAB!" "SCAB!" in unison, amplified.

SCENE SEVEN

Light change. Sound: Church bell. Interior of cottage.
JOAN weeping. ROBBIE enters.

ROBBIE:

Joan. Joan. What is it lass?

JOAN:

Oh thank God you're home.

ROBBIE:

What happened?

JOAN: *(Sobbing)*
Went to church.

ROBBIE:

Aye . . . .

JOAN:

When I sat down they all moved to the other
side of the aisle. Every one of them! As far away
from me as they could get!

ROBBIE:

The bastards! Listen! New miners will be
coming, on the Princess Royal, and that lot will
be gone. Look, Mr. Stuart promised. C'mon, try
and cheer up. *(Pause)* Went out for the first time
with my new prospector's license. Felt good.
Felt free. We'll win out, lass. Wait and see.

JOAN:

No Robbie. I do see. We're cursed here.

ROBBIE:

No lass.

JOAN:

Jamie and Alex will grow up and follow you
down that mine . . . .

ROBBIE:
> Never!

JOAN:
> In twenty years, when they're ready to leave
> home, we'll still be here on this God-forsaken
> island. I see it as clear as I see you. You will still
> be down that damned pit, and there's nothing
> we can do about it. It's God's will.

ROBBIE:
> Joan! That's superstitious rubbish! In two years,
> let alone twenty, we'll have long shaken the
> dust of this place from our boots, you'll see.

JOAN:
> In twenty years you'll still be in pit boots, and
> I'll still be alone in church.

> *Fade sound: Church bell.*

SCENE EIGHT

> *JOAN alone in church — Neutral area. It is twenty
> years later.*

JOAN: *(Wearily)*
> Dear God . . . . Give me understanding. Why is
> it we've had to stay in this town all these years?
> What is Thy purpose? Is it to punish us? Purify
> us? *(Pause)* I beseech you. Be merciful, oh Lord.
> Deliver my men from the mine. Guide us in Thy
> ways. Give me patience with Robbie and his
> wild dreams! Look after James below — and
> guide him in his choice for a wife. And
> Alex . . . give him the strength to stand against
> temptation. I ask this in the name of Thy
> Blessed Son, our Lord. Amen

> *Lights up: Cottage.*

ALEX is sneaking some liquor from a scotch bottle.
He pours some in a glass, and tops the bottle up with
some water. He hears someone coming to the door.
He replaces the scotch bottle and quickly places the
glass with the scotch in it on the sideboard, then exits
upstairs

JOAN enters and looks around.

JOAN:
Is there no one home? . . . Alex?

SCENE NINE

ALEX: *(Entering)*
Just me . . . .

Blast of shift change whistle: JOAN stops and listens.

ALEX:
How was Church?

JOAN:
Same as usual. Where's James?

ALEX:
Probably putting in extra time below . . . he
loves it so.

JOAN:
You take his supper out of the oven?

ALEX: *(Mechanically)*
Sorry.

JOAN looks in oven door.

JOAN:
Ach . . . all dried out. Your father is right
enough at times, Alex. You don't take a thought
for anyone. *(Puts plate on sideboard and then*

25

notices one whiskey glass) Has your father been home and gone out again? Is he with Mr. Hamilton?

ALEX:
    It's Sunday isn't it?

JOAN:
    Stumbling around in the dark and rain.

ALEX:
    Everyone in the village laughing at him.

JOAN: *(Quietly)*
    Do you?

ALEX: *(Flaring)*
    Stop him! You could! Why don't you?

JOAN:
    He does no harm. It may be mad. But it's a madness that keeps him sane. Who laughs at him?

ALEX:
    The lads.

JOAN:
    Which lads?

ALEX:
    Lads below — in the pit . . . they laugh at him behind his back.

JOAN:
    Aye, and that's the only time they'd do it! I don't see why you're so worried. Your father's got YOU a soft enough job above ground . . . and thank God for it.

ALEX:

Aye . . . working with his drunken mate,
"Jug-A-Day Jock." I have to do his books half
the time because he can't see straight. If it
wasn't for Father, he'd have been kicked out of
the mine office years ago. Drives me mad
working under him. I don't know what Father
sees in him.

JOAN:

Your father doesn't have friends by the
bucketful.

ALEX:

None of us do.

JOAN: *(Grunts)*

At least you're out of the pit.

ALEX:

James likes the pit.

JOAN:

Just as well, he has little choice.

ALEX:

James might change his thinking . . . maybe
even broaden his mind . . . reading all these
books Miss Susan gives him. *(Laughs)* Look at
them!

JOAN:

James stepping out with a school teacher. He's a
pit man like his father. If Susan knows what's
good for her, she'll give up on James. Parading
in here with her high and mighty ideas, like my
old Aunt Agnes. Doesn't know the difference
between what she reads in books and what's
real. *(Pause)*

ALEX:

    Here comes the prize student now.

JAMES:

    'Lo.

JOAN:

    Wipe your feet.

JAMES:

    How was Church?

JOAN:

    Same as usual, thank you. I thought you'd be coming home a little less dirty now you're on machines. Give me that shirt. *(She takes it from him)* Yech! Ah well.

JAMES:

    Susan not come for the books yet?

ALEX:

    Doesn't look like it.

JAMES:

    She's got her first class to teach at the mechanics institute tonight. She's nervous as a cat!

JOAN:

    Scrub your nails!

ALEX:

    Been reading this, have you James?

JAMES:

    Which one?

ALEX:

    "A Survey of European Civilization."

JAMES:
Haven't got to that one yet.

ALEX: *(With relish)*
What about: "A Walking Tour of Upper Greece and the Isles of the Agean?"

JAMES:
No.

ALEX: *(Snicker)*
Miss Susan test you on these, does she?

JAMES:
Eh?

ALEX:
Miss Susan examine you regularly, does she? Are you grasping it?

JAMES:
Listen here laddie . . . I'll have your neck!

ALEX:
What have I said?

JOAN:
Don't listen to him, James. Now eat your supper.

Knock at door.

There's Susan.

JAMES rises.

Eat! *(He sits)*
(Mumbling to herself) Wonder what gems of wisdom she's going to impart to all us ignorant souls today?

JAMES:
Mother!

JOAN: *(Opening door — dully)*
> Hello Susan.

SUSAN:
> Hello.

JOAN: *(Alarmed)*
> Put that down! *(Umbrella)* You'll not bring a
> curse into my house with that open!

SUSAN:
> That's just an old superstition, Mrs. Dunsmuir.

JOAN:
> Is that what all these books you bring here are
> all about? To crush ignorant people's
> superstitions?

SUSAN:
> I used to think they would. But now I don't.
> Not after tonight!

JAMES:
> Your night class. What happened?

SUSAN:
> Nothing happened, that's the problem. No one
> came!

JAMES:
> I wouldn't worry, love.

JOAN:
> Ach . . . they're pit men . . . you'll not change
> them.

SUSAN:
> I'm not trying to. The Sunday night class is to
> teach immigrant boys how to read and write.
> I'm not trying to "change" anyone.

ALEX:

>Well don't worry about that night class "lot." Miss Susan, you've got a good student in James here right enough. *(Pause)* James was telling me how much he enjoyed this *(Pause)* Critique of "Hegelian Philosophy of Right." That's right isn't it, James?

SUSAN: *(Pleased)*

>Did you, James?

JAMES:

>Well, I . . . . *(Mouth full)*

ALEX: *(Interrupting)*

>Of course James couldn't discuss the book with me because I haven't read it all yet. I'm just up to this part, when Marx says: "Religion is the opiate of the masses."

JOAN:

>What?

ALEX:

>He says, "Religion is the opiate of the masses!"

JOAN:

>Who said that?

JAMES:

>Well Mother . . . this Marx man. Well, he's, eh . . .

JOAN: *(Interrupting)*

>So is that where our donations to the institute library go? I'll not have things like that said here . . . . This is a God-fearing house, Miss Susan, *(Then to JAMES)* and "the fear of God is the beginning of wisdom."

SUSAN:

>"Walk in honesty — not in rioting and drunkenness on the Sabbath." Isn't that what your Bible says too?

JOAN: *(Sighing)*
Aye.

SUSAN:
And my father and Mister Dunsmuir drinking
out there every Sunday . . . .

JOAN: *(Interrupting)*
There's no good complaining. It's become part
of Sunday, God help us. *(Picking up a coal
shuttle)* You didn't bring in any coal again, Alex.
(ALEX takes shuttle) You finished, James?

JAMES:
Aye. Was a bit "crispy" . . .

JOAN:
Thank your brother for that.

ALEX:
Surprised he noticed, he ate it so fast.

JOAN:
Go on, Alex.

JAMES: *(Smugly)*
Yes. Go on Alex, get the coal.

JOAN:
You too, James, go with him and bring in some
water too . . . .

JAMES:
But Mother!

JOAN:
Go on. Your father will be home any minute
now. I want to talk to Susan.

JAMES and ALEX exit.

Pass me those lunch buckets please. I know how difficult it is for you — your father and my Robbie out there, every Sunday. Rain or shine.

SUSAN:

Getting sloshed! Why do they do it? I would never stay married to a man who . . .

JOAN: *(Interrupting sharply)*
Wouldn't you now?

SUSAN:

NO! I don't know how you put up with it.

JOAN:

And what would you do? You never know what kind of husband God is going to give you.

SUSAN:

No law says I have to marry!

JOAN:

Then I wouldn't if I were you. *(Silence)*

SUSAN:

You don't like me, do you?

JOAN:

It's not that.

SUSAN:

You hope I don't marry James. That's what you want to talk to me about, isn't it?

JOAN:

It's not for me to say. It's up to him.

SUSAN:

But you'd rather he didn't.

JOAN:

No. That's not it.

SUSAN:
  Then what is it?

JOAN:
  It seems to me you shouldn't marry a
  miner . . . and have to make lunches like these.

SUSAN:
  I make my father's lunch every day!

JOAN places the lunches in the buckets.

JOAN:
  But you make a lunch that goes into a wee
  bucket, like this one. This is Alex's,and like your
  father, he's a man works above ground. These
  bigger buckets are for Robbie and James. Y'see if
  you make James' lunch, you'd have to make two
  lunches for him. The first one is to eat . . . this
  second lunch is one a mother or wife prays will
  never be needed. For it's hidden away in the
  bottom of the lunch bucket in case your man is
  trapped underground. When you can make that
  second lunch for James, you'll make him a wife.
  (Sighs) Because, girl, he's a miner, like his father
  and his grandfathers before him, and probably
  his sons to come . . . . You'll not get him out of
  the mine either, no matter how many clever
  books you give him — for it's God's plan . . .
  His way . . . and there's nothing you and I can
  do about it. Would you fetch me some apples?
  (Pause) Last of the fall apples — rest are for
  hogmanay pies. Aye. *(Pause)* So, Miss Susan.
  (Breaking a little) Do you want to be a miner's
  wife? Do you? Do you want your sons to go
  down that Hellhole? Do you want your heart to
  stop every time that mine whistle goes! For if it
  blows on and on, long and mournful, you may
  not have a son or a husband left . . . . *(Pause)*
  It's not that I don't like you Susan. I've known
  you since you were a wee motherless one. But
  you don't want a miner for your man.

(Pause — then understanding) Aye . . . I remember dreaming for better myself. *(Moving away)* But I can't complain — my man may drink too much on a Sunday, but he's his own man. He's kept his family together in this town in spite of everything. And it may be madness that he's out there in the dark and rain, but he's doing it for all of us — that's how he sees it anyway. Besides, it gives his waking hours some meaning, in a place where all meaning's long gone.

JAMES enters with two buckets of water; ALEX enters with the coal skuttle.

JAMES:
>Father's coming.

Door opens. ROBBIE walks in followed by JOCK HAMILTON. ROBBIE has been drinking but barely shows it. JOCK is totally inebriated. ROBBIE eyes them all suspiciously.
They stand for a moment in silence.

ROBBIE:
>Ooh. It's bitter cold out there. Well . . . 'lo all. *(Pause)* Has there been a death in the family?

JOAN:
>Not yet. There's a pot of tea on.

SUSAN:
>We should be going, Father.

JOCK: *(Drunk)*
>Right . . . .

ROBBIE: *(Quickly)*
>We'll not have tea, but we'll have a wee doch-an-doris, eh Jock? I'll pour. *(Pushes JOCK into a chair.)*

SUSAN:
>We should be going.

ROBBIE:
>Just be a minute lass. Now, what about you boys? Aye, well James does not appreciate the benefit — but Alex? (*Shrewdly*) Alex will.

JOCK: (*Drunkenly*)
>Aye, Alex will . . . .

ROBBIE: (*Turning to JAMES and SUSAN to divert attention from JOCK'S condition*)
>And you. I don't know what you're doing standing around here so maudlin. Why aren't the two of you out in the moonlight?

JAMES:
>It's raining out, Father. There's no moonlight.

ROBBIE: (*Tiredly*)
>It's just an expression lad.

JAMES:
>I know.

JOAN:
>What's that?

ROBBIE:
>It's a wee gift for you lass. (*Unveils bell*)

JAMES: (*Shrugging his shoulders*)
>It's a bell.

ROBBIE:
>Aye, James. But not just any old bell. D'you read Joan.

JOAN:
>Pekin. (*Realizing*) The Pekin! (*Delighted*) I thought that old ship had sunk, bell and all.

ROBBIE: *(Grinning)*
> Aye, and it did, but someone saved the bell,
> and when they closed Fort Vancouver to the
> Yankees the Company brought it up here. Jock
> found it in the warehouse.

ROBBIE:
> The last time this bell rang, James, you were
> born.

ALEX:
> I believe we've heard the story, Father.

ROBBIE: *(To SUSAN)*
> Have you heard the story?

SUSAN:
> Yes I . . . .

JOCK: *(Trying to help out)*
> About when you and Missus "D" sailed out on
> a Hudson Bay ship . . . and it ran aground on a
> sandbar, and the ship had to be abandoned . . . .

ALEX:
> . . . and in the excitement of it all Mom had
> Jimmy boy here. *(ALEX reaches out and takes up
> the bottle.)*

JOAN:
> Alex, no.

ROBBIE:
> Why not? It appears we cannot amuse him any
> other way. He's heard all his old father's stories.
> *(Looking around)* Well everyone . . . would you
> like a song instead? Or have you heard all my
> songs too? . . . *(He resumes his Burns Song)*
> Come on Jock! Let's dance!

They whirl around until JOCK collapses.

SUSAN goes to him, everyone is embarrassed.
JAMES helps SUSAN get JOCK to his feet.

SUSAN: *(To ROBBIE)*
> He can't drink like you Mister Dunsmuir — I
> wish he wouldn't try.

ROBBIE:
> James, best see Susan home.

JAMES:
> I know, Father. Goodnight. *(Ad lib.)*

> *SUSAN, JOCK, JAMES exit.*

JOAN:
> No need to tell James what to do. He knows
> how to behave.

ROBBIE:
> Aye he knows how to behave. It's more than his
> brother does. *(Turning to ALEX)* How could I
> breed such different men?

JOAN:
> Robbie, don't start on Alex.

ROBBIE:
> Don't protect him.

JOAN:
> I'm going to bed.

ROBBIE:
> Ach no, lass. I'm alright. C'mon. This is to be a
> special occasion what with finding the bell and
> all. *(Pause)* Let me tell Alex a story he hasn't
> heard.

JOAN: *(Alarmed)*
> What? What are you going to tell him?

ROBBIE:

> Don't worry. This is the story of the first time
> your mother and I heard this bell ring. The wind
> was screaming through the rigging like a
> madman on the pipes . . . we'd rounded the
> Dundee breakwater and we were picked up and
> pitched out into the Irish Sea on a wild tide. I
> was below, crashing and bumping through
> people, piles of luggage and crying children . . .
> *(To ALEX)* looking for your mother. She was
> nowhere to be found. And where were you lass?

JOAN: *(Holding bell)*
> Up top.

ROBBIE:

> Aye, you were out on deck . . . all wet from the
> spray.

JOAN:

> Trying to get one last glimpse of the Scottish
> hills . . . .

ROBBIE:

> Your Scottish hills. And what did I promise you,
> in the wind and rain?

JOAN:

> A castle.

ROBBIE:

> Aye. A castle — a fairytale castle. A castle
> finer . . . *(JOAN and ROBBIE together)* finer . . .

JOAN: *(Alone carrying on the line)*
> . . . finer than those on any loch in Scotland.
> *(She is interrupted when ALEX bursts out laughing)*

ROBBIE: *(Confused)*
> What? What? Are you drunk?

ALEX:
>Your castle. *(Laughing and indicating)* This dump?

ROBBIE: *(Attacking ALEX)*
>Why you — arrogant pup!

JOAN:
>Robbie! *(ALEX stops laughing)*

ALEX: *(Pause) (Then dawning on him)*
>So that's why you do it every Sunday. I thought you were out there looking for some huge motherlode of coal with your "free miner's" license just so you could get rich and free us all from the mine. But you're not. No, *(To JOAN)* he's going out to find you a castle. Going out to keep his promise. *(Slight sneer)* That's what the prospecting license is for.

>*Silence.*

JOAN:
>That's enough, Alex. Your father made the promise to me. It's mine. *(Beat)* He shouldn't have told you about it.

ALEX:
>Why?

JOAN:
>Because you don't understand.

ALEX: *(Angry)*
>Don't I! Well there's one thing I do understand. That bloody free miner's license he got so long ago was too damned expensive. Yes Father, expensive. The price was too high!

JOAN:
>Alex! You've had too much to drink. Now stop!

ROBBIE: *(Dully)*
> No let him go; let him get it out.

ALEX: *(Incredulous)*
> There is nothing to get out . . . except that every
> day . . . every week . . . for all time,
> probably . . . me and James and Mother pay the
> price for you to wander off with your bloody
> prospector's license.

JOAN: *(Going off)*
> I'm going to bed!

ROBBIE:
> Now see what you've done. *(Pause)* No one
> wants to hear all that blather trotted out again.

ALEX:
> Why don't I have a girl, Father? Why?

ROBBIE:
> Uh? A girl? Look at you; sullen, useless lump.
> No girl worth her . . .

ALEX: *(Interrupting)*
> No, Dad. No. Not good enough! There's only
> one girl who'll even talk to me, or James, in this
> village and that's Susan Hamilton. And James
> has her. And why? Because she's your only
> friend's daughter. Why do you think no one
> came to her night class tonight, and no one will
> share the same pew with Mother at Church.

ROBBIE: *(Stung)*
> Enough!

ALEX:
> Why do you think you've never ever been
> invited to the annual Robbie Burns supper in
> town. Because that's the price Nanaimo made
> you pay for your "free miner's" license. Only
> one strike since the mine began, and you scabbed!

ROBBIE:
>Watch your tongue.

ALEX:
>Scabbed! So now we're a scab family. Thanks, Father. Thanks for the leprosy.

ROBBIE:
>Leprosy! You and your words. And that's all they are too . . . words. Look! How many times do I have to tell you? I came here as a servant of the Hudson's Bay Company. They gave us a new life. They deserved loyalty and they got mine. I'm not ashamed of that! Now I won't hear any more on the subject. We'll not talk of it again.

ALEX:
>You just can't wipe it away, Father. It's still part of our lives! *(ALEX slowly rings bell)* "Unclean! Unclean! Unclean!"

ROBBIE:
>You'll not touch Joan's bell! You'll not put your hands on that!

JOAN: *(Entering)*
>Robbie! Robbie! Take your hands off him. You've both drunk too much — now come away.

ALEX: *(Sneering)*
>Why did you let him do it, Mother? How do you put up with it?

>*Silence. JOAN looks at ROBBIE, ROBBIE looks down.*

JOAN:
>Don't be disrespectful to your father. I won't have it.

ALEX:

> You amaze me, Mother . . . .

JOAN:

> Enough!

ROBBIE: *(Upset)*

> At least I believe in something.

ALEX:

> And I don't. You're so right! How can I? I've
> seen how much your ''beliefs'' have cost!

JOAN:

> STOP IT!!

JAMES: *(Enters)*

> It's bitter cold out. *(Pause)* Why is everyone
> taking the huff?

ALEX:

> Don't worry James. Settle down with one of
> your books. It's just another Sunday, and next
> Sunday will be the same. The Chapel bell will
> ring and Mother will come home from Church.
> And Father will be beating around in the bush,
> and we will be waiting for him to come home —
> forever and ever, Amen.

> *He exits.*

JAMES: *(Quietly)*

> Amen. *(As he follows ALEX off)*

> *Silence.*

JOAN:

> Robbie, how much longer do you think this can
> go on?

SCENE TEN

Sound: Church Bells.
JOAN enters from Church, takes off hat and coat,
goes to make tea. Whistle blows a long blast —
emergency! JOAN falls to her knees and prays.
Whistle down.

JOAN:

Dear God — please protect my boy below. Give
him the wisdom to not take chances. Spare him
from danger . . . . And if it is Thy will he be
lost, make his end mercifully quick and give
those of us left above ground the strength to
carry on. For Thy Son's sake, Amen.

Whistle up.
Then she takes pot off stove, dons clean apron. As she
goes to the door, she sees JAMES being carried home.
She sweeps the table clear, puts the pan back on stove
and waits.

JAMES is on a stretcher. They lay him on the table.
JOAN catches her breath.

STUART: *(Quickly)*

He's not dead, Mrs. Dunsmuir, he's not dead.
He's unconscious that's all, he's in and out;
comes and goes, in and out.

JOAN goes for smelling salts.

ALEX goes for scotch.

JOAN puts salts to JAMES' nose, he splutters and
belches up mouthfuls of water. They turn him on his
side.

He'll be fine now. I'd best get back.

JOAN:

Stuart. Thank you.

STUART nods and exits with stretcher. JOAN gives more salts to JAMES. He brushes them aside and sits up. She gets water in pan and begins to wash him as she did with ROBBIE in scene two.

What happened?

ALEX:
He nearly drowned . . . .

JOAN:
Drowned!

ALEX:
He'll be alright.

JAMES: *(Cough)*
Don't fuss, Mother. I'm alright. *(To ALEX)* How's Tommy?

ALEX:
He's going to make it.

JOAN: *(Taking off his shirt, she gasps at the deep scratches on his shoulders)*
How . . . . How did this happen?

JAMES:
Tommy Dean did it. They sent us down to fix the pump in Number Four shaft. When we got down there the shaft was filling up fast with ground water, and we couldn't get the damn pump going. It was up to our knees, so we turned around and waded back to the cage to come up again. It wouldn't go — damn thing runs on this new-fangled steam switch. It's no good — I told them, but old Blackwell won't listen. Then we heard the roof drop further up the drift and the ground water all of a sudden really started coming in. The shaft started filling up like a pint pot. In no time it was up to our necks, and us caught in the cage! I put wee Tommy on my shoulders or he would

have drowned. A minute later we just had *(Shows with his fingers, two inches)* this much space between the water and the top of the cage. Well, Tommy panicked — can't swim see — had to clout him one! As it was — he scratched my shirt off and clawed his finger nails into me. *(Feels around his shoulders)* It was about then they started handwinding us up. *(He continues to feel his shoulders thoughtfully)* Almost too late for Tommy.

JOAN: *(To ALEX)*
Go out to the shed and get that herbal poultice your father used on the horse. I'm afraid its all we have.

ALEX:
Well if it works on the horse, it'll work on James.

JOAN:
Go on. *(ALEX exits)*

Pause.

JAMES:
He's right isn't he.

JOAN:
Eh?

JAMES:
Everyone thinks I'm just a pit pony — all brawn and no brains . . . no feelings.

JOAN:
What are you talking about, James?

JAMES:
When I was stuck below there . . . with the water surging in . . . I was thinking about Susan. In all these months I've never spent any

time with her alone! You know that? We never get to be by ourselves. There's always Alex around, or her father rolling in dead drunk. *(Pause)* Maybe I should get a move on with Susan.

JOAN:

Just because of this bad turn you had below — no need to marry the first girl you've met.

JAMES:

What others am I going to meet? *(Silence)* I'm lucky to have her — anyway — it doesn't change the fact that I never get to see her alone. Not with filling in for Father on Sundays. Is it too much to ask to have a Sunday to spend time with my girl — just the two of us alone?

JOAN:

No. No it's not. I remember . . . when Robbie and I first came . . . we'd sit and talk by the stove on Sunday night . . . *(Wistfully)* seems long ago.

ALEX enters with ointment.

JAMES: *(Rising)*

What's Father doing anyway? He's straining himself six days a week trying to keep pace with the young lads below. Then on Sundays he goes out prospecting for this "magic seam." It's a waste of time, Mother! The company has done hundreds of surveys — if there was anything worth finding they would have found it by now. There's nothing out there!

JOAN:

Maybe you're right — but it's what keeps him going.

JAMES:

He's killing himself working seven days a week.

JOAN:

> Maybe — but it's what he wants to do. I can't stop him.

ALEX:

> He's out there, trying to strike it rich so he can keep his castle promise to you — right?

JOAN:

> I know it's madness.

ALEX:

> Release him from his crazy promise — you're the only one that can.

JAMES:

> Then maybe I'll get a Sunday off for a change.

ALEX:

> And he won't be the laughing stock of the town.

JOAN:

> You don't understand do you? It's not whether he strikes it rich out there — that's not it. It's the hope in every shovelful that keeps him going. Hope! It gives him life! I envy him!

ALEX:

> What about us? Just because you've given up doesn't mean we have to stop living too.

JAMES:

> Mother — Stop him!

JOAN: *(Upset)*

> I can't! If you take his hope away he'll end up like me.

JAMES:

> At least he'll still be alive.

JOAN:

> What d 'you mean . . . ? Still alive.

JAMES:

> He's killing himself — he can't keep it up.

ALEX:

> Lads are betting he won't last two years.
> Heaving around the pit like a wounded mule.

JOAN: *(Unsure)*

> He's alright.

JAMES and ALEX: *(In chorus)*

> He's not.

JAMES:

> He can't keep it up seven days a week. No one
> can. He puts on an act around you.

JOAN:

> Ah. He won't listen! Y'know what he's like.
> Come in here with a belly full of whiskey —
> you'll not reason with him.

JAMES:

> He'll have to listen if we all stand together.

ALEX:

> Yes.

> *JOAN looks doubtful.*

JAMES:

> Yes, Mother.

JOAN:

> I suppose we can try.

JAMES:

> When he comes in we'll tell him. We don't
> budge! *(Bangs his fist on the table)* We'll tell him

there's to be no more of this Sunday nonsense. I
tell you, Mother, if he doesn't stop, I'm movin'
out! He can find someone else to fill in his
Sunday shifts.

ALEX:
And I'm going with him.

JOAN:
No! You'll not do that — you can't!

ALEX and JAMES: *(Together)*
We will!

They hear a noise outside.

JOAN:
That's him.

JAMES:
Remember, we don't give an inch!

*The door bangs open. ROBBIE stands framed in the
doorway. He carries the largest boulder of coal a man
can carry.*

*ROBBIE bangs it on the table, then walks over and
rings the bell. (Pause) Then he roars in delight.
(Pause) They all look at the piece of coal.*

ROBBIE: *(Excited whisper)*
Ten foot thick! Seven thousand tons of coal to
the acre.

ALEX: *(Unsure)*
Ah c'mon, Dad . . .

ROBBIE:
Look! I'm telling you! *(Noticing JAMES)* What
happened to you?

JAMES: *(Going to the coal)*
Nothing. Bit of a dunking, that's all. *(Stroking the
coal)* Where? Where did you find it . . . ?

ROBBIE:

> About a mile from Divers Lake. *(Laughs)* I've been walking over it for years. It was funny — I saw this wee outcrop of coal underneath the roots of a dead alder. Didn't think much of it — but put a rod down anyway. *(Shaking his head)* I couldn't believe it, I put down more rods. *(Excited)* It's the biggest seam of coal I've ever seen!

JOAN begins to cry — then she begins to laugh.

ROBBIE:

> It's true lass. It's ours — all of us. It's Dunsmuir coal. *(Louder, excited)* Are we a clan?

ALL:

> AYE!

ROBBIE:

> Aye. We are. Right lads! Start cutting stakes — make them about three feet long — lots of them. C'mon, let's not waste daylight.

JOAN:

> What about Jock Hamilton?

ROBBIE:

> Don't worry about Jock.

ALEX: *(Dawning on him)*

> It's true, isn't it Dad.

ROBBIE:

> Aye it is.

ALEX: *(Apologetic)*

> I'm . . . well I'm sorry.

ROBBIE: *(Gently)*

> Go lad — be with you in a minute.

JAMES: *(Going off)*
>C'mon Alex.

JOAN:
>Hamilton. Where is he?

ROBBIE:
>I left him at Divers Lake.

JOAN:
>Did you tell him?

ROBBIE:
>Yes, of course. He's my closest friend.

JOAN: *(Sneers)*
>Friend! *(Pause)* Anyway — don't tell anyone else!
>You hear? Tell no one.

ROBBIE:
>I'll have to tell the Company.

JOAN:
>The Company! You must be mad! Why tell
>them?

ROBBIE:
>Well! I can't mine it. I can hardly afford a
>shovel, let alone mine machinery.

JOAN:
>What are they going to give you for it?

ROBBIE:
>Give me? Well . . . a share of the profits, I hope.
>Joan we'll be rich!

JOAN:
>No! They'll be rich. *(Frustrated)* Robbie . . . .
>They don't give the likes of us a share of the
>profit. Ach . . . they may promise you the
>world, but when they have you where they

want you, they'll rob you blind. The time for
dreamin' is over. Now it's time to be practical.

ROBBIE:

But I have no choice! The Company's the only
one with the money.

JOAN:

No. We have to get some money. And start our
own mine.

ROBBIE: *(Bitter laughing)*
Money, from where?

JOAN:

If this seam of coal is as rich as you think it is,
there's bound to be someone who'll invest money.

ROBBIE:

Who?

JOAN:

Diggle . . . is that his name?

ROBBIE: *(Grimly)*
Aye.

JOAN:

You know him from loading the coal.

ROBBIE:

The toffee-nosed prig. He'd spit on me before
he'd talk to me.

JOAN:

He's got money, Robbie. He throws it around
like nothing. Ask any shopkeeper on
Commercial Street. Everyone knows he's rich.

ROBBIE:

Joannie, I tell you . . . . I'd rather die than go
begging to a man like that.

JOAN:

> Robbie, think. You've combed the hills around this town for years, and finally fortune has smiled on you. Now with a bit of enterprise your dream could come true. You go to Diggle. Go up to Victoria and see him cap in hand, and lick his boots if you have to. Here's our chance. Now listen to me, Robbie, you owe it to us — to me; to the children. The boys are right. We've paid too high a price for this as it is! It may cost you some pride but it's cost us all plenty of that over the years.

ROBBIE:

> But Joan . . . .

JOAN:

> Do it, Robbie. I've spent over twenty years patiently standing behind you, believing somehow this misery was what God had ordained for us. But you were right, yes right. Our fate is in our own hands! So let's get on with it. I know how you feel: you've struck it rich — you've succeeded — so let's sell up and get out. But it isn't that easy. We've just begun.

> *ROBBIE stares at her in disbelief.*

> Let's not falter now. You have to go.

ROBBIE:

> Alright! That's if the likes of me can even get to see such a high and mighty creature. *(As JOAN moves to coal)*

SCENE ELEVEN:

Neutral area. DIGGLES' Gentleman's Club.

SMITHERS:

> Lieutenant Diggle.

DIGGLE:
> Yes, Smithers.

SMITHERS:
> Gentleman to see you, sir.

DIGGLE:
> Show him in then, man.

SMITHERS:
> But he's not a real gentleman, sir. Name's Dunsmuir.

DIGGLE:
> Dunsmuir? Never heard of him.

SMITHERS:
> Says he knew you from the coal landing in Nanaimo.

DIGGLE:
> Nanaimo? *(Mystified)* Are you telling me some coal miner wants to see me?

SMITHERS:
> Yes sir.

DIGGLE:
> Bloody nerve.

SMITHERS:
> He says it's most urgent, sir.

DIGGLE:
> Send him away, Smithers. He probably wants money.

SMITHERS:
> No, sir . . . he says he has money for you.

DIGGLE:
> . . . money for me!

SMITHERS:

> Well that's what he said, sir. He wouldn't tell me any more. Said he wanted to tell you.

DIGGLE:

> Bloody nerve of the man. Scottish is he?

SMITHERS:

> Yes, sir.

DIGGLE:

> Where is he? You didn't leave him hanging around the front door?

SMITHERS:

> No, sir. I left him in the cloak room.

DIGGLE:

> Good. Very well. *(Pause)* I'll see him . . . give me money, eh? I'd like to see a Scotsman do that.

> *Light change.*

DIGGLE:

> Money? Bosh! All you've got is some dirt — with stakes sticking out of it.

ROBBIE:

> But the coal . . . .

DIGGLE:

> Is down there and will remain down there — if indeed there's any coal at all!

ROBBIE:

> Now look here . . . .

DIGGLE:

> Have you ever heard of collateral?

ROBBIE:
> Well I . . . .

DIGGLE:
> Possessions — to back a loan.

ROBBIE:
> Well I own the house . . . .

DIGGLE:
> What's it worth? A hundred dollars — three hundred dollars?

ROBBIE:
> Well I don't know it's . . . .

DIGGLE:
> It's worth nothing in terms of collateral. How much do you need to start digging — have you got a figure?

ROBBIE:
> Here . . . I thought eight thousand would do to start . . . .

DIGGLE:
> Eight thousand! Ha! And what do I do if you fail? Sieze your house full of countless snotty-nosed children no doubt.

ROBBIE:
> Now look here.

DIGGLE:
> No, you look here — you've got a few things to learn. Quite a few. Money for me. Huh! We'll see about that! *(Calling)* Smithers! Where is that man? I've got a job for him.

> *DIGGLE exits.*

SCENE TWELVE

Interior Dunsmuir cottage.

JOAN:
You didn't swear at him did you . . . ?

ROBBIE:
I tell you Joanie, I kept my temper and I told
him.

JOAN:
And?

ROBBIE:
You were right. He was very surly and rude at
first, but he soon changed his tune when he saw
how much money he could make. It was funny
really. He called his butler see — I thought he
was going to have me thrown out — but it was
to get him to call in his lawyer.

JOAN:
So you got it drawn up all legal?

ROBBIE:
Aye. *(Producing papers from his pocket)* Just like
you said.

JOAN:
How much is he going to give you?

ROBBIE:
Enough to start. Eight thousand Dollars.

JOAN:
What conditions?

ROBBIE:
Just what you thought. I do all the work and he
takes half the profit.

JOAN:

> It's irresistible to the likes of him.

ROBBIE:

> Aye . . . and on top of that his lawyer says if it's
> not paid back with interest double quick he
> takes the claim and everything we own. It scares
> me, Joannie.

JOAN:

> You'll do it, Robbie. After he's paid back with
> his interest, then what?

ROBBIE:

> He gets half the profits forever.

JOAN:

> Ha! You see what money can mean.

ROBBIE:

> Aye. If you could see this club of Diggles'. If
> you could only see it! I've never seen anything
> like it.

JOAN:

> You mean he asked you in?

ROBBIE:

> No . . . did all our business in the cloak room.
> But the butler let me peek in the doors on the
> way out.

JOAN:

> The day will come Robbie, when the doors will
> no' be closed to you.

ROBBIE:

> The doors have been closed to me all my life.
> (*Holding her*) But maybe that's over and you'll
> have your castle, lass.

JOAN: *(Shaking him)*
> Don't be dreaming now, Robbie — not yet. It's work now. Then maybe there'll be a time for dreaming.

ROBBIE:
> Aye. It's work now.

Act Two

SCENE THIRTEEN

*Interior Dunsmuir cottage. The door flies open and
SUSAN rushes in, followed by an irate JAMES.*

JAMES:
Why couldn't you have waited here?

SUSAN:
You don't know why?

JAMES:
No! Coming to the pit head — carrying on in
front of everyone at ten o'clock at night.

SUSAN:
Yes. Ten o'clock at night. But not just any night.
It's the night of the St. Andrew's Dance — you
promised!

JAMES:
Ach — I clear forgot about the dance. I'm sorry
we're very busy.

SUSAN:
Busy — You're always busy! James, I want to
know where I stand.

JAMES: *(Sits wearily)*
I know.

SUSAN:
I sat at home tonight feeling like a fool in this
new dress. So I decided to let you know what it
felt like.

JAMES:

You succeeded. The lads are still laughing at the Pit Head.

SUSAN: *(Softening)*

I didn't want that. I don't know what I want. I never see you — I don't even see my father. You all dance to the beat of your machines and the sound of your mine whistle. I'm sick of mines and machines . . . and sitting home alone.

JAMES:

It'll be over soon. We have to do double shifts. Even·mother's been doing the ship tallies . . . but the end's in sight. Now our tramway's complete, we can load four ships a day. It'll be worth it. Please be patient, lass.

SUSAN:

Hold me.

JAMES:

I'm covered in coal dust.

SUSAN:

I don't care. *(Sits on his knee)*

JAMES:

Susan, I've got to get back.

SUSAN:

Don't go. Please don't. Let's go for a walk on the beach. There's a full moon.

JAMES:

I can't.

SUSAN: *(Stands)*

Go back then! Go back to your damn pit!

JAMES: *(Gently — exhausted)*
> Ah, Susan . . . . C'mon, I'm too tired for this. *(Sighing)* You don't know how good it feels to sit down.

SUSAN:
> Oh James, I can't breathe in this little town. It's as claustrophobic as any mine shaft. With its rundown school house, and its hopeless children. Week drifts into week, month into another boring month. We plod on. *(Quietly)* Please God dig me out. *(Pause)* Do you understand James?

JAMES is nodding off.

SUSAN: *(She shakes him)*
> James?

Door bursts open as ROBBIE enters.

ROBBIE:
> There you are!

JAMES: *(Waking up with a start)*
> What?

ROBBIE: *(Ignoring SUSAN)*
> James! What the hell do you think you're doing? You've left a full crew standing around at the Pit Head . . . and two trips banked up. We've got to get that hold loaded by midnight or we're stuck with another day's moorage. Come on!

SUSAN: *(Defiantly)*
> It's my fault.

ROBBIE:
> Aye, I heard . . . you're going to have to settle your quarrels outside work hours.

SUSAN:
> There ARE only work hours!

ROBBIE: *(Ignoring her)*
  C'mon James. Alex is up there by himself
  handling things.

Door opens as ALEX enters.

ALEX: *(Cheekily)*
  Hello all.

ROBBIE:
  What the hell's going on?

ALEX:
  I'm hungry! That's what's going on.

ROBBIE:
  You can eat all you want after we've loaded that
  ship . . . now get back to work.

ALEX:
  I'm going to eat, Dad! Eat! It's been fourteen
  hours.

ROBBIE:
  Don't shout. Your mother is in there sleeping.
  You lads could learn from her — she knows what
  work is.

ALEX:
  I can't work if I don't eat!

ROBBIE:
  Eat then, and be quick about it. C'mon, James.

JAMES:
  I'll see you later, Susan, I won't be long.

SUSAN:
  Sure, James.

ALEX:
  Hey Father, I'm told by lads at the Pit that the

village has asked you to be guest of honor at the *(Touch of sarcasm)* Robbie Burns supper . . . *(As ROBBIE leaves)* Will you be too busy to go to that, d'you think? Will you? Will you, Father?

ROBBIE: *(Off)*
Don't worry about that — just get moving.

ALEX: *(Calling)*
Wear your best kilt will you? See all your friends — all your NEW friends. *(Laughs. Takes down the whiskey bottle.)* Well Miss Susan? Going to wear that lovely dress to the Burns supper, d'you think? It will be a grand occasion — the night of the Bonnie Poet — my father. *(Laughs and then drinks)* I wouldn't miss it for the world. *(Drinks)*

SUSAN:
I should be going.

ALEX: *(Holds her arm, then intimately)*
Don't leave . . . please. Here, have a seat.

SUSAN:
I must go.

ALEX:
Susan, please stay for a minute, please. Look at this dump. Nothing has changed! Thousands of dollars pouring in . . . no change. You would think fortune — in the New World — something would change. New house. New horse. Something . . . but no. Look, not even new curtains or pots and pans; everything is as it was. You know why? See, my father — when he buys a new place — it will have to be a castle. Like a castle in Scotland. He won't settle for anything less. Y'know why? Because that old bastard IS STILL in Scotland. He never left! Here in the New World — trees and mountains out there no one has ever seen. But my father and your father — and my mother — even James — they think this is

Kilmarnoch! *(Laughs)* Kilmarnoch! I suppose they
think the Indians are crofters! . . . Incredible! But
you, Miss Susan — you and I — we don't live in
Kilmarnoch do we? Do we?

SUSAN: *(Quietly)*
No . . . no we don't.

ALEX:
Right! We live here! Wherever this is. I was the
first white child born here — you know that? I
come from here — from the strange misty island.
I don't know where it is exactly — but it is not
Kilmarnoch!

SUSAN: *(Bitterly)*
Well, I know where it is! Prison. It's a dark, dank
cell, a cave, just like the mine. It's a place where
even the slightest dream, the slightest idea, is
snuffed out! Nothing will change it! The boys I
tried to teach to read on Sunday nights know.
They know there's no point! They know they'd
be even more wretched than they are now if they
could read books about the real world out there.
They know they can't get out. No more than the
poor pit ponies . . . stabled all their lives below
ground. It would be cruel to show them the
sunlight and flowers above. Better to leave them
in their darkness. *(Catching herself)* I'm sorry. I
don't know why I am telling you all this.

ALEX:
You're telling me because WE don't belong. Do we?

SUSAN:
I . . . I don't know . . . .

ALEX:
My father — when things go wrong — pulls us
into a circle and asks "are we a clan?" and
everyone says "aye!" But I'm not part of his
Kilmarnoch clan . . . . *(Intimately)* Neither are you.

SUSAN:
>What are you doing?

ALEX:
>Please. Please let me hold you. Just for a minute.
>*(Pause, as they embrace)*

SUSAN: *(Breaking away)*
>I can't do this.

ALEX:
>Why? Because of James? He's the pit pony. If you
>want to stay here in this town forever, marry my
>brother. Come here.

SUSAN: *(Uncertain)*
>Alex . . . . No.

>*ALEX gently opens the door*

ALEX:
>There's moonlight out there . . . let's go.

SUSAN: *(Weakening)*
>There's James . . . the mine . . . .

ALEX:
>To hell with the mine. James doesn't have to
>know. Come on.

>*SUSAN and ALEX exit.*

>*JOAN appears from behind the curtain that covers the
>entrance to the upstairs.*

SCENE FOURTEEN

Robbie Burns dinner.

*Sound: Bagpipes. Then hum of voices in a large hall.
Clink of knives and forks.*

MEAKIN:

> It gives me, personally, great pleasure in
> introducing one of our countrymen, at this the
> annual Robbie Burns Supper. He has lived and
> worked in this town since the beginning. He has
> not always been understood. But now I think we
> all see . . . here is a man who is not some far off
> absentee mine owner. NO! He lives and works
> side by side with his clansmen. Like Burns, Mr.
> Dunsmuir is an Ayershire man — so it's fitting he
> should be in the chair of honor this night. *(Pause)*
> Sir, you and your family have brought much
> success and prosperity to our town, and you've
> stayed to share it with us without putting on
> ''airs.''

> *Sound: Murmur of ''HERE! HERE!'' from audience.*

MEAKIN:

> So we salute you along with our nation's bard
> this night. Ladies and Gentlemen, I give you our
> guest of honor, Mister Robert Dunsmuir.

> *Sound: Applause.*

ROBBIE:

> I thank you for those kind words Mister Meakin.
> *(Quoting)* ''O Scocia! My dear, My Native soil!
> For whom my warmest wish to Heaven is sent
> long may thy hardy sons of rustic toil be blest
> with health, and peace and sweet content'' —
> Aye, Robbie Burns — an Ayershire man, like me
> and mine. His heart knew — as mine does this
> night — those three, Health, Peace and Sweet
> Content. And I have YOU, my friends, to thank.
> I am honored. Tonight we remember the words
> of the bonnie poet. He believed in honesty,
> simplicity and toil; work, and the joy and
> rewards of work. These beliefs I share too. When
> I started the Wellington Mine the other owners
> laughed. We were only taking out forty tons a
> day then. But after a wee while we started taking

out four hundred tons a day and they stopped laughing. Since then we've tripled that, and more — and now I have been warned by my competitors that we are shipping TOO MUCH coal and I will glut the market. I say if the market is to be glutted let it be with OUR coal. Aye — for if these far off toffee-nosed owners ever picked up a shovel and did a day's "short walling" we'd "make'm whissle and arms 'n legs and heads would sned like taps o' thristle." But away from that . . . this is not a time to talk of the work we share, but that common heritage we share together. Ladies and Gentlemen, Robbie Burns.

With applause.

SCENE FIFTEEN

Lights up: Dunsmuir house.

ROBBIE:
Ah, what an evening. Did you ever think you'd see the day, Joan?

JOAN:
'Twas a grand occasion alright.

ROBBIE:
Piped in no less, like royalty . . . and old Meakin getting up saying what a pride we Dunsmuirs were to the community — what prosperity we'd brought . . .

ALEX:
"Good Old Meakin" wouldn't speak to us a year ago.

ROBBIE:
I'm in no mood for your sarcasm. Anyway, there'll be no dampening of spirits this night. Come over here, Joan. Come lad. Let's drink a toast . . . .

JOAN:

> More toasts? Ach. Let's wait for James and Susan at least. I'll put on the kettle.

ROBBIE:

> It'll maybe take a wee while for them to get old Jock to bed. *(Pouring)* Aye, he's a good man and all . . . fine form tonight.

ALEX:

> Fell off the table.

ROBBIE: *(Sharply)*

> At least HIS heart is in celebration! *(ALEX grunts)* Joannie, I've got something to show you.

JOAN:

> What?

ROBBIE:

> It's for you. On this the happiest occasion of my life since the night we wed.

JOAN: *(Softening)*
> Oh Robbie. What is it?

> *Sound: Unwrapping the picture.*

ROBBIE:

> Open it, you'll see . . . .

JOAN: *(A little excited)*
> Are you not going to wait for the others?

ROBBIE:

> No, it's better we heard about this now. *(Lifting and holding up)*

JOAN:

> A castle.

ROBBIE:
> I had an artist paint it — from builder's plans.

JOAN: *(Taken aback)*
> Builder's plans . . . . Look Alex . . .

ROBBIE:
> You'll have your castle in this life . . . that's what
> I promised, and that's what I'll deliver.

ALEX:
> So . . . plans all made up. Where will it be built
> — this castle? Here, in Nanaimo? Or will it be in
> Kilmarnoch?

ROBBIE:
> It will be built where Joan wants it built. *(Aside to
> ALEX)* I'd like to build it on the High Street, in
> Kilmarnoch, right next door to that mean man.
> *(To JOAN)* I've named your castle, Joan.

JOAN: *(Gently)*
> What? You and your dreamin' . . . what have
> you called it?

ROBBIE:
> Craigdarroch . . . aye, Craigdarroch. The
> birthplace of Annie Laurie . . . .

> *He sings a verse of "Annie Laurie" to JOAN. It is
> interrupted when SUSAN and JAMES enter.*

JAMES:
> God what a noise. Still at it? *(Pause)* What's this?

ALEX:
> Mother's castle.

JAMES:
> Eh?

ALEX:
> Dad's going to build it for her.

JAMES:
> I don't believe it.

ALEX:
> Builder's plans made up and all.

JOAN: *(Tantalized a little)*
> Just your father dreamin' . . . .

ROBBIE:
> Not a dream — a reality — soon as we get the
> new shafts producing. Craigdarroch will be a
> tribute to your mother. *(Elated)* Are we a clan or
> no'? . . . Aye we are! Here's to your castle, Joan.
> *(Holding up the picture)* May these sturdy walls
> and stone keeps shelter you. *(To lads)* For I
> promise you — it'll be built to last . . . as a
> tribute to your mother and "R. Dunsmuir and
> Sons," and their sons and daughters for
> generations to come. *(Grandly)* Aye, the
> cornerstone will be laid — one year from this
> night.

JOAN:
> Oh Robbie . . . .

ROBBIE:
> Craigdarroch! *(All toast)* Let's not stand maudlin.
> What's the good of a castle if there's no light or
> merriment in it? . . . I'll tell you what it is — it's a
> ruin. Only fit for "Bogles" and ghosties! And
> we'll not have that. So a tune, let's have a tune.
> *(Begins clapping and humming a piper's tune)* Come
> on now . . . come on Joan. Alex! Where are you
> going, Alex? *(Pause)* Well never mind. *(Pause)*
> James! Dance with your mother! Go on, make
> yourself useful. C'mon — don't just stand there
> lad . . . dance! I'll provide the music.

SCENE SIXTEEN

Interior kitchen area.

ALEX and SUSAN alone in the kitchen.

SUSAN: *(Pause)*
Is there something wrong?

ALEX: *(With sarcasm)*
Oh no. There's nothing wrong.

SUSAN:
Look I'm sorry if I've upset you.

ALEX:
What do you mean, sorry?

SUSAN: *(Shrugging)*
Just sorry, that's all.

ALEX: *(Tremble in his voice)*
Look at me. *(Pause — then suddenly)* Why? Why!
Tell me why.

SUSAN: *(Defiantly)*
Why what?

ALEX: *(Anguish)*
Ever since that night . . . .

SUSAN:
Nothing happened.

ALEX:
Nothing. Is that what you call it? Why don't you
look at me? Why won't you talk to me? Been weeks!

SUSAN:
I can't! I just want to forget that night. I'm sorry
— now let me go.

ALEX:

    Go where? Back in there to James? You just
    want my brother so you can be part of the
    Dunsmuir clan. *(Pause)* You're like everyone else.
    Patting the successful Dunsmuirs on the back.
    You don't want my brother — you want me — me!

SUSAN:

    Let go of me!

ALEX: *(Hissing)*
    You're like me!

SUSAN:

    I can't. *(She breaks off from him and re-enters the
    front room)*

SCENE SEVENTEEN

    Banging at door, but it goes unnoticed.

DIGGLE: *(Entering)*
    Good evening.

    The singing dies, the dancing stops in mid step.

ROBBIE:

    Mr. Diggle.

DIGGLE:

    I am sorry to disturb you.

ROBBIE:

    This is . . . unexpected . . . . *(Pause)*

DIGGLE:

    I am sorry. *(Pause)*

ROBBIE:

    Well then. This is my wife, Joan. My two sons,

Alex and James; Susan Hamilton . . . . Lieutenant Diggle.

DIGGLE:
>Had natives canoe me up from Victoria. Beggars were very tardy on the oars . . . should have been here earlier. Realize this is unexpected.

JOAN:
>Can I get you some tea, Mr. Diggle?

DIGGLE:
>No, thank you. Look here, Dunsmuir . . . can we talk? In private?

ROBBIE:
>I'm sure . . . Joan, er, boys . . . .

DIGGLE: *(Bluffly to JOAN)*
>It concerns business, Mrs. Dunsmuir.

JOAN:
>Then it concerns me, Mr. Diggle.

DIGGLE: *(Appealing)*
>Mr. Dunsmuir?

ROBBIE:
>She's right. There's no one in this room who need leave.

SUSAN:
>I should.

ROBBIE:
>Stay, Susan . . . you're family. Now, sir?

DIGGLE: *(Uncomfortable)*
>I'm afraid I have bad news.

ROBBIE:
>Thought as much . . . care for a dram?

DIGGLE:
>No, thank you. Dunsmuir, I have confirmation from the market in San Francisco that the price of coal has dropped markedly! *(Pause)* Damn it all . . . ! You have only yourself to blame. Over production! You've glutted the market! Your coal is sitting in huge piles on the San Francisco docks. No one will give you more than ten dollars a ton for it. I may know nothing about digging coal, but I can read a balance sheet.

ROBBIE:
>Aye. You can read that alright — done well off it too. Made a pretty packet, while us lot have been splitt'n our back bones below. It's always the way.

DIGGLE: *(Ignoring him)*
>My lawyer has instructed me to have you . . . sign over . . . . I simply cannot risk my continued support . . . .

JOAN:
>You're telling us we're ruined.

DIGGLE:
>I'm afraid you are . . . yes.

ROBBIE:
>Ruined! We're only ruined because you don't have the spine to carry on in the heavy weather. You're a High Street nitwit with the spine of a boiled carrot.

DIGGLE:
>I don't have to listen to this! *(He goes to exit)*

JOAN:
>Wait on, Mister Diggle. How much do you want?

DIGGLE:

I don't think I've made myself clear. You have glutted the market and the present price of coal will not support continued production. And you . . . er . . . Mr. Dunsmuir has no financial leverage.

JOAN:

Cash!

DIGGLE:

Cash — to sustain things . . . .

ROBBIE:

We've invested our earnings in new shafts, you know that!

DIGGLE:

Which are singularly untenable . . . er *(To JOAN)* . . . not worth going on with.

JOAN:

And you want to take what you can and get out.

DIGGLE:

This is business.

ROBBIE:

Business! Open the door, James — something stinks in here.

JOAN: *(Squares off)*

Shut up, Robbie! It IS business, Mister Diggle! HOW MUCH?

DIGGLE:

You don't understand.

JOAN:

Oh yes I do! How much to buy YOU out?

DIGGLE: *(Hedging)*
>Our competitors have offered me four hundred thousand dollars for the works and the machinery.

ROBBIE:
>Christ!

JOAN:
>Then we'll give you six hundred thousand.

ROBBIE:
>We can't!

JOAN:
>We can and we will!

DIGGLE: *(Flabbergasted)*
>How can you?

JOAN:
>Give us six months. Diggle, you've nothing to lose — you can always foreclose.

DIGGLE:
>Well . . . I . . . .

JOAN: *(Pause)*
>Six hundred thousand. Not a bad return on your eight thousand dollar investment. *(Pause)* It's up to you . . . but we need six months!

DIGGLE:
>I can only wait three months — no longer.

JOAN:
>Three months it is then.

>*Pause. DIGGLE finally nods in agreement.*

JOAN:
>I'll have the papers drawn up tomorrow. Do you have a place to stay, Mr. Diggle?

DIGGLE:
>I have rooms at the Oxidental. Thank you.

JOAN:
>James — see Mr. Diggle to his hotel.

JAMES:
>Yes, Mother.

SUSAN:
>I must get home to Father.

ALEX:
>I can see Susan home.

JOAN:
>No! . . . no, we need you here, Alex. Go ahead James — Susan will be with you in a moment.

DIGGLE:
>See you. Tomorrow. Good evening.

ROBBIE: *(Dully)*
>Oh . . . aye.

>*DIGGLE and JAMES exit.*

ROBBIE: *(When door is closed)*
>Tomorrow. Huh! What tomorrow?

ALEX:
>Nice turn of events. I'll get your cape, Susan.

JOAN:
>I'LL get Susan's cape. Get the books and tallies in order, they're on my bureau.

ALEX: *(Angry)*
    Right! *(Exits upstairs)*

SUSAN:
    I must go.

JOAN:
    Just a moment. Susan, James can wait on a
    minute. *(Darkly)* You've seen and heard things
    tonight as family.

SUSAN:
    You don't seem pleased.

JOAN:
    Susan, there's a storm coming . . . and you're
    going to have to make up your mind.

SUSAN:
    I . . . . What do you mean?

JOAN: *(Cutting her off)*
    You're either clan or no'. *(Pause)* Here. *(Cape)*
    (Brusquely) We need Jock! Please ask your father
    to come here first thing in the morning. We
    need to audit our books . . . .

JAMES: *(Re-enters)*
    Mr. Diggle is growing impatient.

JOAN:
    Go then. Goodnight, Susan.

SUSAN:
    Goodnight.

    *JAMES and SUSAN exit, as ALEX returns to the
    room with the account books.*

ROBBIE: *(Picking up the picture)*
    So much for your castle, Joan. *(Puts it down)*
    We're finished, ruined . . . six hundred thousand!

JOAN:

> We've got three months.

ROBBIE:

> Might as well be three million years. Ah. WHAT can we do!

JOAN:

> First thing is to send someone we can trust to San Francisco, and find out what's happening to our coal.

ROBBIE:

> Who? Who can we trust?

JOAN: *(Looks straight at ALEX)*

> I'm going to bed. Don't be long.

> *JOAN goes off.*

> *Silence: As ROBBIE goes and picks up the picture of the castle again.*

ALEX:

> Father?

ROBBIE:

> Aye.

ALEX:

> Mother's right. Someone should go down to San Francisco to see what's going on.

ROBBIE:

> That so? Who do you have in mind?

ALEX:

> Me. Let me go.

ROBBIE:

> You'd like that wouldn't you. Get out before the ship sinks.

ALEX:

> Send me to San Francisco and I'll save the goddamned ship! And that's a promise!

SCENE EIGHTEEN

> *Sound: Mine whistle.*

JOAN:

> How long is this going to take?

JOCK:

> As long as it takes.

JOAN:

> How long's that?

JOCK: *(Cheerfully)*

> Don't boil your water, Missus.

JOAN:

> I beg your pardon!

JOCK: *(Pointing to stove)*

> Your water's boiling.

JOAN:

> It's a wonder you can see the page after last night.

JOCK: *(Coolly)*

> Missus — I know when it is time to dance — and I know when it is time to work. Just let me get on with it.

JOAN:

> Tea?

JOCK: *(Disgusted)*

> Tea. Nooo — No tea.

ROBBIE: *(Off)*
Well?

JOCK:

Patience lad. Just about there. *(Mumbling)*
. . . Capital interest — six hundred . . .
thousand . . . carry over . . . . *(Pause)*

ROBBIE: *(Entering)*
Got it?

JOCK:

. . . checking . . . thirty-two point seven . . .
make it thirty-three.

JOAN:
Thirty-three? What?

JOCK:

. . . percent. Thirty-three percent. There it is.
(Pause) Have to cut your overhead by thirty-
three percent and continue to produce the same
amount of coal, and you'll survive . . . just.

ROBBIE:
Where do we cut? Our overhead has been pared
to the bone as it is. There is nowhere to cut!

JOCK:
I don't know about that lad. But there are the
figures . . . and that's what you're going to have
to do. Cut thirty-three percent!

ROBBIE:
Thirty-three percent . . . .

JOAN:
Only one place to cut.

ROBBIE:
Where?

JOAN:

Wages. Cut your men's wages!

ROBBIE:

But thirty-three percent!

JOAN:

It's the only way.

ROBBIE:

A lot of those men are friends.

JOAN:

If they're friends, they'll understand.

ROBBIE:

Y'know Jock, I could ask the men maybe . . . to take a wee cut . . . they're decent reasonable men. Be only till things pick up. I'm sure they'll understand — look at the bonnie supper they gave us.

JOCK:

What if they won't go along with you?

JOAN:

They live in houses we built — we'll evict!

JOCK: *(Shaken)*

Robbie? Surely no'.

ROBBIE: *(Confident)*

Won't come to that. We're Scots. Brothers. Go and tell them I'll be down in a minute . . . . Aye, they're good men. They'll understand. Don't worry. *(Seeing JOCK out the door)*

JOAN:

When ARE you going to stop dreaming? Scots? Brothers? The only time they clanned with us was when it suited them. Before that, they spat at us on the street — and they'll do it again, so we'd better be prepared.

ROBBIE:

> How?

JOAN:

> If the evictions fail. Threaten them with black leg
> labor.

ROBBIE:

> I'd rather go back down to the pit.

JOAN:

> But you can't go back there — none of us can,
> even if we wanted to. Can't you see that. Too
> much has happened. We've got to be prepared
> to act. If the threat of black leg labor fails — cut
> off their credit at the stores.

ROBBIE:

> I won't watch them starve.

JOAN:

> It's their choice.

ROBBIE:

> What happened to the bonnie Joan I married?

JOAN:

> You changed her. Long ago you promised her in
> the New World there would be a new beginning
> — that her sons wouldn't have to dig coal until
> they were spitting it from their lungs. The
> bonnie Joan you married didn't believe it then —
> now she does.

ROBBIE:

> Working below, pit men learn to stick together.
> You'll see. They'll take the cut. *(Pause)* You'll
> see.

> *Sound: Cat calls.*

> *Lights change.*

SCENE NINETEEN

ROBBIE: *(Calling across stage — to MEAKIN who has appeared in neutral area)*
>Lads, it's only temporary. You have my word on it!

MEAKIN: *(Shouting above the rest)*
>Your word! You'll never change Dunsmuir.
>You've got a scab heart and YOU'LL NEVER
>CHANGE. May you rot in Hell! For we'll not
>save you — or your mine! Trying to profit off
>the backs of your clansmen! We have one
>answer, right boys! Boooo!

Sound: Mass booing.

MEAKIN: *(Motioning for silence)*
>Alright lads. Away you go to your wives and
>family — we'll stay and pick off any scabs.

SCENE TWENTY

Interior of house. ALEX enters from upstairs.

ROBBIE: *(To JOAN and ALEX)*
>They booed and *(Hurt)* jeered me.

ALEX:
>Probably indigestion from that Robbie Burns
>dinner they gave you.

ROBBIE:
>I mean . . . it's as if . . . they thought I did it
>deliberately — out of spite. They booed . . . then
>up and walked off — quit!

JOAN:
>They've had their chance. Now evict them.

ROBBIE:
>But their families . . . .

JOAN:
>Families. Huh! We were a "family" here once.
>Evict the lot. Unless they go back to work at the
>new wage.

ROBBIE:
>I can't.

JOAN:
>They're your houses! You've got to break them!
>Robbie — when are you going to realize this is
>business. Not a matter of what's good or bad,
>right or wrong. It's business.

ROBBIE:
>Business! Throwing families out on the street?

JOAN:
>US or them!

ROBBIE:
>We can't.

JOAN:
>We can and we will!

ALEX:
>— Ah . . . "Long may thy hardy sons of rustic
>toil be blest with health, peace and sweet
>content." *(Laughs)* Ooooh . . . indigestion.

JOAN:
>Enough! *(Beat)* There's a storm coming sure
>enough. Don't you see? It's them or us!

SCENE TWENTY-ONE

Neutral area.

*MEAKIN and another miner appear. They see JOCK
approaching them.*

MEAKIN: *(To MINER)*
> Ooh, do you see who I see? Struttin' down the street.

MINER:
> I do. It's no less than "Jug-A-Day" Jock! Man of importance, a friend and advisor to the rich and mighty one.

MEAKIN:
> It's true what you say, Charlie. *(They stand aside — and doff their caps — then bow.)* Wonder if he's taken a cut in his wages?

MINER:
> Hey "Jug-A-Day" — you takin' the cut?

MEAKIN:
> Being reasonable — with the governor? Are you?

JOCK:
> I am and if you had any brains you'd do likewise.

MEAKIN:
> That so "Jug-A-Day?" Maybe you're well enough healed these days to not miss one-third of your pay packet, but us poor pit ponies aren't.

MINER:
> I bet your "Mr. Dunsmuir" and his "Mister Diggle" won't be takin' no cut in profit.

MEAKIN:
> True ain't it "Jug-A-Day?"

MINER: *(Grabs JOCK from behind — then grabs JOCK'S belt and begins to tighten it)*
> Profit is like pants. If they starts to drop, tighten the belt!

MEAKIN:
>His pants! Our belts!

JOCK:
>You don't understand!

MEAKIN: *(Temper rising)*
>DON'T I now? I tell you what I do understand. I understand that we're livin' on bloody potatoes at home — my two boys have had to be pulled out of school. And it's breakin' their mother's heart. 'Cos she knows they'll end up like me now — scramblin' in the cold and dark, a thousand feet below — and not knowin' whether they'll see the sun again. And I understand — we're lookin' at bein' thrown into the street, next thing.

JOCK:
>He won't do that — I know him. You'll find if you're reasonable, he'll be reasonable. God — he knows what it's like to work below.

MINER:
>That's what we thought — and we worked our hides to the bone to get him started. Then the bastard turned on us again.

MEAKIN:
>Always said he'd do this, Charlie. Once a scab, always a scab!

JOCK:
>You're wrong about him. He's a reasonable man. I'll stake my life on it!

>*They release him and begin to exit.*

MEAKIN: *(Calling after him)*
>Well, we'll see — he'll have his chance soon enough.

MINER: *(As they begin to exit in the opposite direction)*
  Should have tightened it around his bloody
  neck!

SCENE TWENTY-TWO

Interior Dunsmuir house.

SUSAN:
  I couldn't see any harm in trying to help.

JOAN:
  I don't need your help!

JAMES:
  But Mother . . .

SUSAN:
  Mrs. Dunsmuir, you're a mother and the wife of
  a miner. How would you like to be evicted?
  These women came to me, with a petition to
  give you — a petition to be reasonable.

JOAN:
  Stay out of it.

JAMES:
  Seems fair though . . . outside arbitrator.

ROBBIE:
  We don't need outsiders.

JOAN: *(To JAMES)*
  Don't you see, James, if they bring in an
  arbitrator, it could take weeks. Then he might
  rule against us!

SUSAN:
  But they want it settled quickly — they told me.
  Not just the wives but the men as well — only
  they're too proud to ask.

JAMES:
Could try . . . .

SUSAN:
Everyone could be back to work!

JOAN: *(Firmly)*
The evictions will go ahead!

SUSAN:
No!

JOAN:
Stay out!

ROBBIE:
To survive — we have to start producing at the low wage now.

SUSAN:
But those people. Mr. Dunsmuir . . . .

ALEX: *(Snickers)*
I don't see why everyone's so upset. We're only going to be slightly less popular than we've ever been.

SUSAN:
It's not funny! We must do something!
(Appealing) James?

JAMES: *(Appealing)*
Mother . . . . Not eviction.

SUSAN:
There must be some other way! More decent.

JAMES:
Yes.

JOAN:
Don't YOU get on the subject of decency.

SUSAN: *(Flaring)*
> Why? They're working people, like us. How can you expect the loyalty of your workers, if you're not loyal to them?

JOAN: *(Grabs the petition and tears it up)*
> And don't talk to us about loyalty, Miss Susan! Not you!

JAMES:
> Mother!

JOAN:
> Listen James. Your little crusader here — your Joan of Arc — your little Miss Susan — ask her about her loyalty to YOU.

SUSAN:
> What?

JOAN:
> Night of the St. Andrew's dance.

JAMES:
> Eh?

JOAN:
> With Alex!

SUSAN:
> You're an evil woman!

ROBBIE: *(Interrupting)*
> Here now . . . .

SUSAN:
> Nothing happened that night. Nothing. Alex! Tell him! Alex!

ALEX laughs.

JAMES:
>Why you rotten little bastard. I'll kill you!

A scuffle ensues.

JOAN:
>Stop it! Both of you!

ROBBIE:
>We're in enough trouble out there — without this! Step back! Step back! *(Pause)* Now cool down.

JOAN:
>Alex, get packed! You're going to San Francisco. Do something besides stir up trouble!

SUSAN:
>Him stir up trouble! . . . .

JOAN: *(To SUSAN)*
>And you. Get out!

The door bursts open.

JOCK: *(Breathless)*
>Robbie. The sherriffs are out there dragging women and kids out on the street. You gave me your word! Your word! You can't do this . . . you were in the mines once yourself man.

JOAN:
>And now he's out of it — and he's staying out! We have no choice.

ROBBIE:
>None.

JOCK: *(Pause as he studies ROBBIE for a moment then seems to realize something)*
>By God you will. I never thought I'd see the day

when I'd be at war with you, Robbie Dunsmuir, and I tell you, it's a war you're asking for.

JOAN:

So the worm turns!

JOCK: *(Ignoring JOAN)*

Robbie, they're not violent men out there. But if you start throwing them out on the street with nothing and no hope . . . .

JOAN: *(Interrupting)*

They've lived with nothing and no hope for generations. They'll live now, but WE'LL NOT go back to that. And don't be talking of war here. Or you'll be the next to be evicted, you ungrateful sot. If it wasn't for Robbie, you'd have been thrown out of the mine into the gutter years ago!

ROBBIE: *(Weakly)*

Joan . . . .

JOAN:

Don't Joan me! It was him that said cut a third! *(To JOCK)* Where did you think the cut would come from — you mindless dolt!

JAMES:

But Mother . . . . *(He fades off at JOAN's withering look)*

SUSAN:

Call yourselves men! Look at you! Driven by this mad woman. Clan with you — I couldn't. Not with her!

JOAN:

Get out! The two of you!

SUSAN:

Come on, Father.

JOCK:
Aye. God help you, Robbie Dunsmuir.

JOAN:
Good riddance to them. James, you're best off without her. She's no clan of ours!

ROBBIE:
It's a bitter wheel turning. What's happening to us?

ALEX:
Nothing new, Father. Nothing new.

MEAKIN: *(Off)*
Hey Dunsmuir! Robert Dunsmuir!

ROBBIE:
Is that Meakin? James, can y'see?

JAMES: *(Looking out the window)*
It's Meakin.

MEAKIN: *(Off)*
Dunsmuir!

ROBBIE: *(Yelling)*
Speak your mind.

MEAKIN:
We're giving you one more chance. Stop the evictions and sit down and bargain with us in good faith or else!

JOAN: *(Yelling)*
We'll not be threatened by you, John Meakin.

MEAKIN:
Can you not speak for yourself, Dunsmuir? Or are you hiding behind your woman's skirts!

ROBBIE:

> I won't be intimidated by the likes of you!
> (*Pause*) You've heard our offer! We'll not back
> down!

MEAKIN:

> I warn you, scabby! We'll give you forty-eight
> hours, and then if you are bent on putting us
> down, so be it! But we'll take your mine down
> with us! (*Pause*) Right boys! Give him a taste of
> what's to come . . . .

> *Sound: An explosion. Followed by a series of
> explosions.*

JAMES:

> They're blowing up the track.

ROBBIE: (*Furious — going to the door*)

> Soon sort this out!

JOAN:

> Stop Robbie! Robbie! Robbie. Don't go out
> there.

ROBBIE:

> I must!

JOAN:

> Let them blow up all the track! Listen to me!

ROBBIE:

> But Joan . . . .

JOAN:

> Don't you see — now's our chance. They've
> broken the law. Now I'll go to Victoria. Alex
> YOU'LL escort me. And then go on to San
> Francisco. This is the chance we've been
> waiting for!

ALEX:

>Amen!

>*To black as lights come up on neutral area and DIGGLES' Gentleman's Club.*

SCENE TWENTY-THREE

>*Diggles' Club — Neutral area.*

>*Sound: Buzz of conversation. Clink of glasses.*

SMITHERS:

>Madam . . . you can't come in here. Gentlemen only.

JOAN: *(Entering with ALEX)*

>Get out of my way!

SMITHERS:

>Madam . . . .

JOAN:

>Mr. Diggle.

DIGGLE:

>Mrs. Dunsmuir. Dash it. You can't come in here.

JOAN:

>Diggle, listen and listen now.

DIGGLE:

>Can't we talk about this elsewhere?

JOAN:

>In the cloakroom, I suppose. Get off your backside, Diggle, and get your military friends together, or you won't have a mine to foreclose on! It's being torn apart!

DIGGLE:
>I beg your pardon?

JOAN:
>They have explosives down there!

DIGGLE:
>Oh my God!

JOAN:
>Diggle, you get going. We're in trouble!

DIGGLE:
>Come!

>*DIGGLE leads them off.*

SCENE TWENTY-FOUR

>*SUSAN stands in the neutral area. JOCK enters —
>He has obviously been searching for her.*

JOCK:
>What are you doing? I told you to stay in the
>house!

SUSAN:
>I went to watch the sheriffs and bailiffs
>upholding the law and the "rights of property"
>of our former friends.

JOCK:
>Aye — Who did they evict?

SUSAN:
>Oh, they were very brave — they only picked on
>the homes where they knew they wouldn't get
>their noses broken. The first was Mary Arnot's
>— you know her, her husband was killed a year
>ago in the Wellington. Mary had to send her
>eleven-year-old into the pit so she and her other

children could stay in the company house. They soon drove her and her children out. One of the little girls was sick, so they dumped the mattress with the child still clinging to it into the street. The oldest boy tried to stand up to them and they kicked him unconscious. I tried to stop them but they threw me aside. Then they went to work throwing everything out of the door. Pots, plates, clothing. They even uprooted Mary's vegetable garden so her family had nothing left to eat. The others, barricaded in their homes, watched, waiting for their turn. Finally some of the men couldn't stand it any longer and went to her aid. At first — only two men . . . but soon others joined them. They threw anything they could lay their hands on till the sherriffs turned and fled. When it was over, a strange silence fell. Then suddenly they let out a cheer, it echoed down the streets. It felt good to be there. I found myself cheering too.

JOCK:
Better not cheer too soon. The militia began disembarking at Departure Bay an hour ago . . . .

SUSAN:
Where are you going?

JOCK:
To warn Meakin and the others.

SUSAN:
Let me go with you.

JOCK:
No, stay. It's getting dark. I won't be long — go straight home!

SUSAN:
Please let me come with you. (JOCK pauses, then nods — they exit)

Sound: Riot — Then gunfire.

SCENE TWENTY-FIVE

Interior house — A noise is heard outside.

JOAN: *(Unnerved)*
Who is it . . . . Eh?

JAMES: *(Looking out through the barricaded window)*
It's Susan.

JOAN:
Susan?

JAMES goes — and removes the barricade from the door.

SUSAN: *(Enters. She is wide eyed — she looks almost deranged)*
Don't touch me James. Don't anyone in this house touch me. They're all going back to work — you've won. *(Pause)* But there was a price. *(Breaking)* This was my father's . . . .

ROBBIE:
His cap. It's all covered . . .

SUSAN: *(Interrupting)*
. . . in blood. He's dead! Shot! Got in the way, the captain said. True too, isn't it Mr. Dunsmuir?

ROBBIE: *(Breaking)*
. . . Jock . . . . Not Jock!

SUSAN: *(Recoiling) (Pause)*
You are scabs, all of you, aren't you? And once a scab always a scab . . . always. Using people. Crushing those in your way until there's no one left to crush but each other. That's next! Isn't it? Each other!

100

JOAN:
Crush each other? You'll not bring a curse on us!

SUSAN: (Quietly)
No. You're already cursed . . . . All of the people that you've crushed and betrayed for this (Points to the picture) will come back to haunt you. This (Picture) will be the death of your "clan." (Directly to them) You'll end up eating each other alive! Wait and see.

She throws JOCK's cap at the picture, leaving a trail of blood on the canvas.

SUSAN: (Off)
Goodbye, James.

She exits.

JAMES: (He exits after her)
Susan . . . Susan . . . . Wait!

JOAN:
The way she looked at me . . . .

ROBBIE:
I wish I'd never found it. I do! I do!

JOAN:
You mustn't say that!

ROBBIE:
Look at all the misery it's caused. She's right! I am cursed by this.

ROBBIE smashes the picture.

JOAN:
No!

ROBBIE:
An outcast when I was born. Met you, and

made you one! Then made my whole family lepers when I came here with my pigheaded desire to prove something to your father by getting ahead . . . building you that! *(He breaks)* But now the cost . . . poor old Jock . . . .

JOAN:

No, Robbie. No! You've never done anything unless it was for us. Don't lose sight of your dream. Don't falter now. You can't. NOT NOW. Can't you see that. *(Pause)* My castle.

ROBBIE:

Aye?

JOAN:

Don't let it die, you worked too hard for it . . . don't give up . . . now it's so close. Tell me. Tell me what it's going to be like. Please Robbie, tell me!

ROBBIE:

Tell . . . ?

JOAN:

What will it be like? Come on, take me to my castle. What would I see?

Pause.

ROBBIE:

The first thing you'd see . . . .

JOAN: *(Gently encouraging)*
Yes . . .

ROBBIE:

The first thing . . .

JOAN:

Would be . . . ?

ROBBIE:
>A tower, aye, a tower, a strong tower built of granite with porte cochere and stained glass windows, crowned with a spired roof — stretching from the keeps, and as you got closer, Joan . . . in your coach . . . you would pass the first lodge, guarding the grounds. Soon you would arrive at the marble steps . . . cross lightly over the mosaic-tiled veranda into the great entrance hall, with its mahogany fireplace, oak-panelled walls — and the light — light, creeping down like gentle fingers from the myriad of stained-glass . . . stretching up . . . up over the circular balconies on every level . . . whispers of red, blue, purple, gold . . . light from the curved stained-glass above. A festival of soft . . . light . . . to . . . dance . . . .

JOAN:
>Dance . . . ?

ROBBIE:
>Yes . . . the double doors on the last level of the spiral staircases open onto a ballroom, bathed in chandeliers . . . more light . . . illuminating the ceilings hand-carved and painted in Florentine figurines . . . and . . . as the music cascades in concert with the light of the chandeliers high above . . . bathed in showers of light and music . . . . Down below we are dancing . . . dancing . . . in your . . . . *(He's holding back the tears)*

JOAN:
>Castle.

ROBBIE:
>Aye.

OPTIONAL *The exterior of the castle magically appears (possibly through a scrim by means of rear projection).*